The Time Traveler's Guide

Writing time travel stories and historical fiction

By

Simon Rose

The Time Traveler's Guide
Copyright © 2016 by Simon Rose

Published by Sorcerer's Letterbox Publishing
Calgary, Alberta
www.simon-rose.com

Contents

Introduction

This book explores the creation of time travel stories and examines the writing of historical fiction. Books are always able to transport us to other places and this is certainly the case with stories involving time travel or those set in a different historical era.

Stories featuring time travel inevitably overlap with other genres. Authors of novels involving journeys into the past have to contend with many of the issues faced by authors of historical fiction. Stories involving time travel into the future or into alternate timelines have many things in common with complex science fiction adventures.

My novels *The Alchemist's Portrait, The Sorcerer's Letterbox, The Heretic's Tomb, The Time Camera, Flashback,* and *Future Imperfect* all feature time travel. Although these novels are written for young adults many of the themes explored in the following chapters are also applicable to those authors that are writing for adults.

This book examines the definition of time travel and historical fiction, along with the creation of imaginary yet plausible time travel machines, methods, and devices. Each chapter explores the appeal of certain historical eras for time travel stories, the importance of historical research when choosing a setting, creating characters and crafting dialogue, stories featuring travel to the future, and the genre of alternate history. Common mistakes and issues related to writing about time travel are also covered.

Chapter One
What is time travel?

Time travel is defined as taking place when there is movement between specific points in time. This is achieved in the same way that objects and living things move through space. In fiction, this kind of travel is made possible by the use of a time machine, device, or method. While nothing is carved in stone, I tend to think that time travel involving machinery or some kind of technology should be defined as science fiction while time travel that makes use of magic or similar methods is probably best classified as fantasy. However, these genres frequently overlap, particularly with time travel stories.

Over the years, novels, movies, and TV shows featuring time travel have included methods involving highly sophisticated machinery, scientific laboratories, various items of jewelry, wearable technology, vehicles, ancient artifacts, books, portals and doorways, dreaming, food and drink, and so many more. Time travel stories have featured journeys to the past, the future, and to alternative timelines created when previous events were changed so that they occurred differently, thus affecting what happened next in various different ways. Time travel has long been a theme in books, short stories, TV shows, and movies and shows no signs of declining in popularity anytime soon, although of course only time will tell.

A common theme in time travel tales involves someone being sent into the past by accident. When they arrive at an earlier point in history, the device or machine is somehow broken, fails to operate properly, runs out of power, is misplaced, or is stolen by the story's villain. The reader is thus left in suspense, wondering if the heroes will be able to return safely to their own time. Of course, the reader most likely believes that the heroes will eventually escape from danger. However, the plot still has to imply that the lead characters might be marooned in the past permanently or that their lives are in jeopardy. In my time travel novels, the main characters always face serious challenges from the moment that they appear to be trapped in a dangerous historical era.

Some time travel stories simply feature an adventure in a different period in order for the characters to experience what life was like. Perhaps the character discovers an old piece of jewelry that sends them back in time when they wear it or adjust it some way. The characters then witness historical events or meet famous people. Many time travel stories concern the consequences of travelling either backward or forward through time. The idea of changing the past, either intentionally or by accident, is a common theme in science fiction and fantasy. When events that have already taken place are altered in some way, what the time traveler knew as the present day has changed when they return home. This might lead to a further adventure to restore things to what's perceived as normal, depending on the nature of the alterations to the timeline. As you're probably thinking already, time travel can sometimes be very complicated but the creators of these kinds of stories are aware of the potential issues at the outset and work hard to make their story entertaining, plausible, and realistic. Some stories in the genre concentrate on the paradoxes involved in time travel, such as the well-known grandfather paradox. This is when the time traveler is responsible for the death of his or her own grandfather, meaning that the traveler was never born. If this is the case then how could they have gone back in time to cause their grandfather's death in the first place? Time travel has lots of issues like this, some of which I examine in Chapter Nine.

Time travel stories involving journeys into the past overlap with the genre of historical fiction. This kind of fiction involves stories that are set in the past. There are no firm rules, but the setting is usually at least fifty years earlier than when the story is written. The setting is a particular period in history and often includes real historical personalities. The story's main characters are usually fictional, although the social and other conditions of the time are presented accurately. Historical fiction stories usually take place during a significant period in history. In some stories the characters are part of the events taking place but in others the events merely serve as the background to the story.

In *The Sorcerer's Letterbox*, the story takes place in 1483 and features the aftermath of the Wars of the Roses and the mystery of Edward V and Richard, Duke of York, known as the Princes in the Tower. The princes appear in the story, as does their uncle, King Richard III, along with some other historical characters. In *The Heretic's Tomb*, the story takes place during the period of the Black Death in England in the mid fourteenth century. The novel features imaginary characters but also refers to the effects of the Black Death on society, medieval medicine, and living conditions, and to some of the personalities and events of the era.

In *The Alchemist's Portrait*, Matthew's time travel adventures take him to Amsterdam in 1666, the French Revolution in 1792, the American Civil War in 1865, and the Russian

Revolution in 1917, all of which needed to be portrayed accurately. *The Doomsday Mask* has scenes that take place in Berlin in May 1945 and the characters needed to fit into that world. In *Flashback*, Max finds himself in the mid 1990s, not too long ago perhaps, but he still needed to inhabit an environment that's correctly portrayed. Next, we'll look at some of the many time travel stories that have appeared in printed form and on screen over the years.

Chapter Two
Time travel stories

When you think about time travel stories that have appeared in movies, novels, and TV shows it's surprising how many there have been. The idea of using a mechanical device to travel in time first appeared in H. G. Wells' 1895 novel, *The Time Machine*. In the story the inventor designs his machine and uses it to travel hundreds of thousand of years into the future. Charles Dickens explored time travel in *A Christmas Carol*, published in 1843. Ghosts visit Ebenezer Scrooge and show him the future. Perhaps this is not strictly time travel since the traveler doesn't physically journey to another time. However, Scrooge does witness what lies ahead, or might do, if he doesn't change his ways, so his knowledge of the future certainly affects how the story progresses. Mark Twain also featured time travel in his 1889 novel *A Connecticut Yankee in King Arthur's Court,* in which a nineteenth century man journeys back to the time of King Arthur in early medieval England.

The *Star Trek* franchise has used many different methods of time travel both in movies and in the various TV series. In the original series, *The City on the Edge of Forever* involves traveling back to Earth in the 1930s to put events back on track in order to save the future. In *All Our Yesterdays* Kirk, Spock, and McCoy are trapped in another planet's past. *Yesterday's Enterprise,* in the third season of *Star Trek: The Next Generation,* along with the final episode in the series, *All Good Things*, also featured time travel, as did *First Contact*, the second movie featuring the *Next Generation* cast. There have also been time travel episodes *in Deep Space Nine, Voyager*, and *Enterprise*, as well as in the 2009 *Star Trek* movie featuring characters from the original series.

Dr. Who also first appeared on TV in the early 1960s. The Doctor travels through both time and space during his many adventures but the

TARDIS is still a type of time machine. *The Time Tunnel* was on TV in the late sixties around the same time as the original *Star Trek* series. In the first episode the two main characters were trapped aboard the *Titanic* and were then sent to a different time period in each installment as they tried to return to their own time. A similar concept was explored in the TV series *Quantum Leap* in the early 1990s. A time travel experiment causes the main character to be trapped in the past. He then temporarily becomes other people as he attempts to return to what he knows as the present.

In Kurt Vonnegut's *Slaughterhouse-Five* the main character travels erratically through time, moving randomly from one event in his life to another. Being lost in time with seemingly no control also features in *The Time Traveler's Wife*. In the novel the main character's genetic disorder causes him to experience his life's events in a random order as he travels though time. In my first novel, *The Alchemist's Portrait,* Matthew's time travel adventures take him to Amsterdam in 1666, the French Revolution in 1792, the

American Civil War in 1865, and the Russian Revolution in 1917, as he struggles to get home.

Many people are very familiar with the story of *Back to the Future* and the time travel method involving the DeLorean and the flux capacitor in the adventures in which Marty McFly travels back to the 1950s, encountering his parents before they first met, jeopardizing his own existence since he risks never being born. In the second installment Marty journeys into the future in memorable scenes featuring hoverboards, flying cars, and futuristic technology, as well as to the Old West in the third movie.

J K Rowling included time travel in the third novel in the Harry Potter series, *The Prisoner of Azkaban*. The time-turner is depicted as a small hourglass on a necklace. The number of hours the user wishes to travel back in time is determined by the how many times they turn the hourglass. At the end of their trip when the hourglass in fully emptied the travelers automatically return to the present, a concept used in other stories. In Rowling's novel there's also an implication that there's a limit to how many times someone can travel to the past. The time-turner also doesn't allow a traveler to spend days and weeks in another time. Hermione originally employs the device to help her cope with her studies but later in the novel the time-turner is used by her and Harry to save Sirius Black and the hippogriff, Buckbeak. In the novel, the characters also take care not to see or meet their other selves in the past. This element has featured in other time travel stories and is covered in more detail in Chapter Nine, which examines some of the issues commonly faced by writers of time travel stories.

Time travel to a specific historical period in which the characters must take great care not to alter events also appears in Michael Crichton's *Timeline*, in which archaeologists undertake a journey to medieval France. The time travel method and equipment are incredibly complex, but still appear perfectly plausible to fans of the genre. Two of my time travel novels are set in the medieval era. In *The Sorcerer's letterbox*, Jack travels back to the Tower of London in 1483 using a wooden box through which he's able to receive messages from Edward V, one of the

Princes in the Tower. In *The Heretic's Tomb*, Annie uses a mysterious amulet to reach the era of the Black Death in 1349.

In some stories, the main characters somehow obtain knowledge of the events to come or are contacted by people from the future. A few stories have involved characters reading future newspapers and attempting to alter the existing timeline. In the movie *Frequency* from 2000, a man uses a radio to connect with his father who died thirty years earlier and attempts to save his father's life. In my tenth novel, *Future Imperfect*, Alex and Stephanie receive communications warning them of what lies ahead. The messages also offer advice regarding how Alex and Stephanie can take action in their own time to prevent a terrible future from becoming a reality. In *The Time Camera*, Magnus Sinclair uses the camera to view the future and profit from it in his own time to make himself rich. Jake and Lydia also attempt to use the camera to try to save Lydia's mother who died years earlier.

There have been countless examples of time travel in the superhero genre in comic books, TV shows, and movies. The X-Men saga, *Days of Future Past*, was adapted for the screen in 2014 and involves altering the past so that a deadly war with the X-Men's formidable enemies the Sentinels never begins. Wolverine's mind is sent back into his younger body but he retains his memories of the future and is capable of influencing events back in 1973.

The concept of altering the past to affect the future has been employed frequently in time travel stories. However, although the motivations of the characters are often very noble, changing past events usually has consequences, both good and bad. The butterfly effect, which states that even tiny changes to the timeline can have a huge impact on the future, is covered in more detail in the Chapter Nine. In the 2004 movie *The Butterfly Effect* a college student uses his journals to travel into his younger body, but the seemingly simple changes that he makes drastically affect what he knows as the present. In the Ray Bradbury's *A Sound of Thunder*, travel to the time of the dinosaurs must follow strict safety procedures and when these fail or are ignored the future is catastrophically transformed.

In the 1994 movie *Timecop*, a police officer employed by the Time Enforcement Commission prevents people from using time travel to change the past. However, the officer is also tempted to use time travel himself to save his late wife. In *Looper* from 2012 Bruce Willis appears as the main character's future self. In the mid twenty-first century time travel is controlled by organized crime and hired killers execute people delivered to them by means of time travel. Bruce Willis also appears in *12 Monkeys* (1995) as James Cole, who travels to the mid 1990s to prevent the outbreak of a deadly virus that killed billions and is an established historical fact in his own time.

Travel from the future to either alter history or to ensure that events occur is also a central theme of the *Terminator* movies. In the first movie the cyborg played by Arnold Schwarzenegger is sent back in time from 2029 to 1984 to kill the mother of John Connor, the man that will save the world in a future war against machines. In the second installment the cyborg is sent to 1995 to protect the young Connor from another terminator, while in part three people in the future make a final attempt to kill Connor as an adult.

There have been a number of comedies that feature time travel as part of the plot. In the 1986 movie *Peggy Sue Got Married* the main character is living in an unhappy marriage and is visiting her high school reunion when she passes out. She wakes up at an earlier point in her life near the end of her time in high school. Based on her knowledge of the future she attempts to change her life. In 1989's *Bill & Ted's Excellent Adventure,* the two teenagers need to achieve an A in their history project in order to graduate from their high school. With the help of a time traveler they journey through the centuries, meeting a number of historical characters. In *Hot Tub Time Machine* from 2010, the characters find themselves in 1986 and try to alter their fates.

Although machines and magic are most often featured in time travel stories, another method is suspended animation, in which people are frozen or enter a deep sleep, awaking decades or sometimes centuries later. This method is used in Robert Heinlein's *The Door into Summer*, in which the lead character is trapped by suspended animation for thirty years. When he finally awakes he's able to use time travel to get even with those that betrayed him. Suspended animation also features in the original *Star Trek* episode *Space Seed*, in which the character of Khan Noonien Singh was first introduced. Even Washington Irving's *Rip Van Winkle* involved the character going to sleep for an extended period and waking up in the future.

Time travel has often featured in children's literature. In *The Missing* series by Margaret Peterson Haddix famous children are stolen from different time periods by time travelers from the future. In the *Magic Treehouse* series, the main characters use a magic book to travel to a different time in each adventure. Their destinations include the dinosaur era, the Ice Ages, Ancient Egypt, Medieval England, Pompeii, the Renaissance, the time of King Arthur, and many more. In *Tom's Midnight Garden*, a boy lives in an apartment in what used to be a large country house. At night Tom is able to visit the house's beautiful garden from the late nineteenth century, where it's daylight and he plays with a girl his own age.

So many time travel stories have already appeared but although one story might easily be influenced by something else, time travel remains one of the most fascinating genres. It has endless possibilities and its own set of challenges in order to make the story plausible but a time travel story will always be a lot of fun to write.

Chapter Three
Creating your time machine

There are over five thousand recorded years of history to serve as an inspiration for writers in many different genres. Time travel adventures and historical fiction stories show no signs of waning in popularity, but to be believable to the reader, even stories involving magic or imaginary technology have to be grounded in reality. Although you may have selected a year or time period in which to set your story and have most of the plot details worked out, the key element is still the method of time travel. This has to be extremely well thought out and also appear plausible to the reader. Yes, it's a fantasy story but it's crucial that your time machine, method, or device, whether it is mechanical, magical, or even supernatural, seems to be authentic in the mind of the reader.

In my first novel, *The Alchemist Portrait*, the idea was originally a story about a ghost inhabiting someone's painting. Instead, the novel developed into a story about someone being trapped inside the painting by an evil spell or curse. Once I'd decided that a character would rescue the prisoner from their portrait I began thinking more about the painting itself and this changed the story into a time travel adventure. In the novel, Matthew is on a field trip with his school to the art gallery at the local museum. When he places his hand on the canvas of the portrait of Peter Glimmer, a seventeenth century Dutch boy, Matthew's hand sinks into the painting, like quicksand. He can also step through the frame and actually be inside the picture. From the inside, he can see the museum gallery that he just stepped out of, complete with other museum visitors, although they're unable to see him. From the inside, the portrait's frame is also capable of showing images from all the different time periods wherever the painting existed in the past. Just as Matthew can step into the painting from the outside, he can also step from the inside into any of the historical eras displayed within the frame. He then travels back not only to when the painting was first created in 1666 but to the French Revolution, the American Civil War, and the Russian Revolution.

Matthew is only able to travel to one of the time periods when the painting was hanging on the wall in the past. Travel to the dinosaur era or to the Middle Ages isn't possible, since the portrait has only existed since the 1660s. Hence travel can only take place to time periods since that date and also only to places where the portrait was located since Matthew uses the frame as a doorway. A simple idea maybe, but how does this doorway actually work? Although time travel may remain firmly in the realm of fiction, the conditions under which it occurs still have to be believable. If readers consider your means of time travel to be utterly ridiculous, they will quickly be turned off the story altogether. If the process is described in a way that makes the time travel method appear workable to the readers, the concept will be sound. Although the story in *The Lion, the Witch and the Wardrobe* involves travel to another world rather than into different time period, we don't question that four children can walk into a wardrobe and reappear in Narnia. Similarly, the fact that Alice can tumble down a rabbit hole into an underground dimension or that a flying boy outside the window can lead his young friends to Neverland, seems perfectly reasonable in the imagination of the young reader. In *The Alchemist's Portrait*, Matthew is able to travel in time through the use of magic rather than by employing a complex device with a number of buttons, switches and dials.

Magic also plays a role In *The Sorcerer's Letterbox*, in which Jack travels to the late fifteenth century on a desperate mission to save the Princes in the Tower from Richard III. When Jack discovers an old medieval wooden box, he's able to write letters on a scroll placed in the box's drawer. Jack is astonished to be corresponding with King Edward V, imprisoned in the Tower of London in 1483. Inside the box is a mysterious wheel, which Jack must twist anticlockwise to journey into the past. Although the wheel and the box could be classified as a crude machine, magic is the means by which Jack travels to 1483.

Although my fourth novel, *The Emerald Curse*, doesn't feature time travel, Sam uses a magical pen decorated with a green gemstone to travel into a comic book universe. Sam's grandfather, Charles Kelly, used the same pen to create his superhero stories and artwork before he mysteriously disappeared. To enter the comic book world Sam draws images of himself into copies of the panels that appear in one of his grandfather's stories.

A time travel method needs to be well thought out in the mind of the writer. Imagine if a plastic water bottle was your time travel device. A key question is whether it's the water or the bottle that has magical powers. This is a simple query perhaps but still one that's very important to clarify. If the water is magical it presumably needs to be consumed by the traveler to enable them to travel through time. So what happens when the water runs out or evaporates or is otherwise no longer around? The character is then trapped in the time period to which they

25

traveled. However, if the bottle is the story's key element then this can have the power to transform any liquid placed inside it into a magical potion. The main character can then put anything into the bottle to recreate the time travel method. This makes the idea fully believable for the reader.

The water bottle example also stresses the importance of a time travel device's portability. In *The Alchemist's Portrait* Matthew uses the painting's frame as a doorway but in *The Sorcerer's Letterbox*, Jack takes the box with him on his journey back to 1483. In *The Heretic's Tomb*, Annie wears the mysterious amulet when she finds herself in the era of the Black Death in 1349. A large time travel device makes it difficult for the character to carry it with them. Sometimes the time machine might be safely hidden in another time to prevent the people of that era from finding it, as occurs in the third installment of *Back to the Future* when the car is concealed in a cave in the Old West. Yet there's always a possibility that the device might be found, damaged, or even stolen, even if the thieves don't fully understand what it is.

Consequently, small items that can easily be carried or concealed usually work better, unless the story involves time travel for a limited period or the travelers have a device that makes a portal appear when it's time to go home. Time travel employing jewelry, such as rings, bracelets, or necklaces, also works well. These are often magical or at least have a mysterious history and of course are also able to be carried by the character. You also need to be careful about the power source of your imaginary device. In many time travel stories this is rarely mentioned, especially if the device is magical in nature. If it's something that's usually charged somehow in the present day, this could create insurmountable problems if its power becomes exhausted in the past. Consequently the author needs to pay special attention to this aspect of the chosen method of time travel.

In *The Time Camera*, Jake and Lydia travel into the past using a digital camera, changing the date when they take a picture. However, they don't spend long enough in the time period that they visit for the camera's power source to be an issue. In *Future Imperfect*, the only time travel involves messages from the future delivered via a mysterious app on Alex's cell phone. This is plausible because the method was invented in the future in order to send messages back to our time. Since fictional future inventions are always fair game, it's very feasible that someone using advanced technology could send these kinds of messages and keeps the story rolling along nicely.

In some time travel stories people might fall asleep or get knocked unconscious and wake up in another time. These are common enough methods that are often combined with another feature, such as a character being in an old historic building before falling or banging their head on something. Or perhaps they're reading a book or looking at a picture of a certain historical period before falling asleep. Yet unconsciousness by itself isn't enough and the reader will you inevitably question how this imaginary time travel method really works. In *Flashback*, Max goes back into someone else's life with the help of a psychic who uses hypnosis to send him on his way. Max eventually returns to his own time by the same method but only after desperately searching for the same disbelieving younger psychic in the earlier time period, confessing his true identity so that he can travel home safely.

In my creative writing workshops on this topic, the majority of children generate wonderfully inspired ideas related to time travel, but some struggle to explain how their machines or methods actually function. The children are also usually very clear on the way their character travels back in time, but have given little thought to the return trip. This element has to be plausible too, unless a person is escaping to the past or intends to stay there for some reason. This is why jewelry and other small items work well since the traveler can usually retain possession of these relatively easily in order to go home at the end of their adventure.

In the time travel genre, people often undertake journeys in both time and space. Rather than travel from their hometown to the same location in a different time, they go to Ancient Egypt or the Middle Ages in Europe or to

World War II in the Pacific and so on. The idea that the time machine stays in one place hasn't been used as often by writers but was featured in Wells' *The Time Machine.* Once activated, the Victoria apparatus that the main character sits inside remains in place as the surrounding area rapidly changes with the passing centuries.

Even though your story is set in a different time period, the reader still needs to believe that the events depicted could have really happened. Many readers of historical fiction and time travel stories have favourite eras and know a considerable amount about the period, whether from their own reading and research or from other novels with similar settings. As a result they'll always be very quick to notice and indeed perhaps point out errors or unbelievable elements in your work.

Obviously the author needs to conduct research into their chosen time period, whether this involves weaponry, clothing or living conditions, as well as the personalities and events of the time. If you don't have the luxury of visiting archaeological sites and museums to conduct research in person, there are plenty of places online where this information can be studied. This includes contemporary accounts written by people who lived at the time that can go a long way toward you really getting to grips with what life was like in your chosen historical period. We'll examine this in more detail in the chapter dedicated to historical research.

However, it's not all about description or even getting all your facts straight when it comes to historical eras. Even though you've spent your life in the modern age, it's important to try and put yourself into the mind of your characters and imagine how they'd have viewed their world and reacted to everything around them. If you can accurately recreate the time period in which the story takes place the reader will get a true sense of place. If readers really feel like they're living in a medieval castle, watching the pyramids being built, walking the streets of Victorian London, or viewing the preparations for a Napoleonic naval battle, the author's done a successful job.

Chapter Four
Settings and historical eras

Time travel stories involving journeys into the past generally feature eras that readers will be familiar with. The world in which the story takes place, as well as the actual timeline of events in the story, whether used as part of the plot or just as background, needs to be accurate.

A number of different factors are involved in the selection of a setting. As well as the time and place, you might want to select a period that's interesting to you. If you choose something that seems to be popular but in which you have little interest, the whole writing and researching experience could be a lot less enjoyable. Having said that, it's sometimes advisable to select a well-documented period so that the research is a little easier.

In terms of location, the best place to start is to

think about an area of the world that you're interested in. It could be the town, city, or country where you live, or perhaps you've always been fascinated with England, Egypt, China, India, Scotland, France, Japan, Ireland, South America, the Middle East, it's really up to you.

Is there a particular time period that you're interested in? Ancient Greece or Egypt, the Roman Empire, the Vikings, the Middle Ages, the Aztecs and Incas, the Renaissance, the Tudors, Victorian London, World War I, for example, are all popular time periods. Most of these are very well documented. This means that there's a lot of information available to use in a story but it also means that you have to be very careful in your research and can't deviate too far from historical facts. A less popular time period gives the writer more opportunities to modify events. However, there are usually fewer sources to rely on and readers will be unfamiliar with your topic. Your story might also focus on a specific event, such as the Crusades, the Black Death, the Spanish Armada, the French Revolution, the American Civil War, the Russian Revolution, or World War

II. You then need to decide if events will form the main part of the story or will only be in the background.

History is divided into many different eras. There are also some very familiar characters, such as Robin Hood, pirates, or highwaymen that are associated with certain historical periods. Some historical time periods have been used many times as settings for time travel stories and continue to be popular.

Ancient Egypt

This is a lengthy era divided into a number of different periods from around 3000 BC until Egypt became a Roman province in 30 BC.

Ancient Greece

This tends to overlap with other eras, but usually runs from around 500 BC until Greece was conquered by the Roman Empire in 146 BC.

The Roman Empire

The empire existed for more than 500 years until 476 in the west. The eastern part of the empire survived as the Byzantine Empire well into the medieval period.

The Dark Ages

This term used to refer to Europe after the fall of the Western Roman Empire in the late fifth century until around the year 1000. It is also known as the Early Middle Ages.

The Vikings

A popular topic for historical fiction, the Viking Age in England and Europe dates from 793 to 1066.

Medieval

A time associated with kings and queens, castles, warfare, knights, chivalry, and feudalism. The medieval era comprises the Early (500 to 1000), High (1000 to 1300), and Late Middle Ages (1300 to 1500). The medieval period is usually defined as ending at the beginning of the Renaissance.

The Crusades

This most commonly refers to the medieval wars fought in the Eastern Mediterranean. European armies fought against the Islamic rulers of the Holy Land in a series of crusades from 1095 to 1291.

Robin Hood

Robin Hood is usually depicted as living in the north of England during in the reigns of Richard I and John from 1189 to 1216. However, the legends are probably more accurately placed in the reign of Edward I and Edward II in the late thirteen and early fourteenth centuries.

The Hundred Years War

This was mostly fought in France between English and French armies from 1337 to 1453. Joan of Arc was a leading figure in the later years of the conflict.

The Wars of the Roses

This conflict in England between the House of Lancaster and the House of York for control of the English crown took place in the second half of the fifteenth century.

The Renaissance

The Renaissance is usually depicted as beginning in Italy in the second half of the fifteenth century and spreading to other parts of Europe until the early seventeenth century.

The Reformation

This occurred in the Renaissance era, from 1517 until the mid-seventeenth century.

The Age of Discovery

This usually refers to the era after Columbus' discovery of the New World in 1492. It also includes the European voyages to other parts of the world and the Spanish conquest of the Americas.

The Tudors

In England, this dates from 1485 to 1603. Many historical novels set in this time period focus on the reigns of Henry VIII and Elizabeth I

Elizabethan

This refers to the reign of Elizabeth I of England from 1558 to 1603.

The English Civil War

The conflict between Charles I and Parliament in England in the 1640s.

Restoration

This is the period following the return of Charles II to the throne of England in 1660 until 1685.

Pirates

The most popular pirate stories take place in the late seventeenth and early eighteenth centuries. These are usually set in the Caribbean, although pirates did also operate in other parts of the world.

Highwaymen

The mounted robbers of stagecoaches in England are mostly associated with the eighteenth century.

The American Revolution

This period usually covers the later decades of colonial America and the Revolutionary War in the late eighteenth century.

The French Revolution

This is a popular topic for historical fiction and covers the period in France from 1789 to 1799.

The Napoleonic Wars

Following the rise of Napoleon, these wars took place between France and the other leading powers of Europe from 1803 to 1815.

Regency

The Regency began when the Prince of Wales took over royal duties from the seriously ill George III in 1811. Regency era stories often cover the time of the Napoleonic Wars until the 1820s.

The Industrial Revolution

This period dates from the late eighteenth century to the middle years of the nineteenth century in Britain, parts of Europe, and North America.

American Westward Expansion

This usually covers the first part of the nineteenth century until the Civil War when settlers moved west. It can also include the later period when settlers were in conflict with Native Americans.

American Civil War

Novels set in this time period often feature the decades leading up to the conflict in the 1860s.

Victorian

The period during the reign of Queen Victoria in Great Britain from 1837 to 1901.

Edwardian

Britain in the first decade of the twentieth century during the reign of Edward VII.

Colonial

This usually refers to the period from around

1870 to the end of World War II, when European countries controlled large areas of Africa and Asia.

The Great Depression

The economic downtown that was first felt in the United States in 1930 and spread to other countries. It lasted for much of the decade before World War II.

The Inter-war Period

This covers the 1920s and 1930s between World War I and World War II.

Whatever time period you choose, make sure it's one that you're truly interested in and remember to carry out enough historical research so that your depiction of the era is accurate and is able to generate a vivid picture in the mind of the reader.

Chapter Five
Historical Research

Even though your time travel story is a work of fiction, if it's to remain credible for the reader, all the historical details featured in the story must always be accurately researched.

In *The Alchemist's Portrait*, Matthew's travels through the painting displayed in the museum take him to Amsterdam in 1666, the French Revolution in 1792, the American Civil War in 1865, and the Russian Revolution in 1917. I conducted research into many aspects of all these historical periods, including clothing, lifestyle, scientific knowledge, weapons, and the events of the time. I also studied the art of seventeenth century Amsterdam, including paintings such as *The Laughing Cavalier* and other works by Frans Hals. Some of these were very helpful in describing the era's clothing correctly and inspired some of the characters that appear in the novel.

In *The Sorcerer's Letterbox*, Jack's adventure takes place in late medieval England. The discovery of a letter in the drawer of a mysterious box leads to Jack connecting with Edward V, one of the Princes in the Tower of London, before becoming trapped in 1483. The Wars of the Roses that took place in England in the mid-fifteenth century can be very confusing and hard to follow due to the many people involved in the fighting. Although the story in *The Sorcerer's Letterbox* takes place at the end of the conflict, I still needed to do extensive research into this turbulent era, as well as into the mystery of the Princes in the Tower, the disappearance of the two boys, and the imposters that later appeared. I studied everyday life in the late Middle Ages, what people wore, ate or drank, maps of medieval England and the city of London, as well as the language spoken at the time. This wasn't English as we know it today but Middle English and although the characters speak in a way that can be understood by the reader, it was vital that the scroll that Jack discovers in order to initiate the adventure was written in the appropriate language. The message Jack receives had to be composed in the alphabet and style of Middle English as it would have been spoken in the 1480s.

The novel features Richard III, Edward V, and other historic characters, so it was important to conduct research into their activities and locations when they appear in the story. For example, if Richard III is shown entering a room at the Tower of London on a certain date in 1483 it was vital to know that he was in the area at that time and not out of the country or in a different part of England. With regards to the Tower of London, I needed to be certain about the layout of the complex and its grounds, including which buildings would have existed or been in regular use in 1483. All of this was crucial to creating a plausible image of the time period described in the story.

The Heretic's Tomb is set during the time of the Black Death in the mid fourteenth century, when more than twenty five million people died of the plague throughout Europe. When Lady Isabella Devereaux obtains a mysterious amulet, she soon realizes that it has the power to bring those that have recently died back to life. Lady Isabella plans to use the artifact to cure the great plague but Sir Roger de Walsingham has other plans for the amulet, which will help him to seize the Kingdom of England.

The novel involved researching fourteenth century England, the Black Death, and its impact on the country and elsewhere in Europe. As in *The Sorcerer's Letterbox*, my description of Middle English had to be accurate, but *The Heretic's Tomb* also features a Latin spell book, so this language had to be depicted correctly as well. I also researched the Hundred Years War, the reign of Edward III, medieval cities, villages, houses, and castles, as well as monasteries, abbeys, and the operations of the medieval church. It was important for me to know about the history of printed books, scrolls and manuscripts, since these appear in the novel. Some parts of the story also take place in the present day at an archaeological site and this had to be described accurately for the reader as well.

Although I ensured that I was describing the horrors of the Black Death correctly, I also needed to research medical treatments that would have been available in the mid-fourteenth century. This was important since Lady Isabella is a physician and any treatments she employs when conducting her medical work had to be in keeping with her era. In the following chapter I examine medieval medicine and the medical knowledge and treatments that were available at the time of the Black Death, which played a part in what I included in the story.

The plot of *The Doomsday Mask* involves the ancient city of Atlantis, lost civilizations of the Americas, theories about mass extinctions, and end of the world prophecies. These elements involved considerable research but I also had to get things right for a particular historical era. The beginning of the novel takes place in Berlin in 1945 at the end of World War II. The story also features items such as gold, silver, artwork, and jewelry that were looted from all across Europe throughout the war and hidden by the Nazis. I researched the many stories about stolen treasure, hiding places, and how much of the priceless loot was recovered at the end of the war. I read extensively about the fighting in eastern Germany as the Soviet armies approached Berlin. I also conducted research into the desperate battle for the city and what daily life would have been like for Berliners at that time. The two children that appear at the beginning of the novel were both recruited as soldiers despite their age. I needed to make sure that my depiction of these boy soldiers was accurate, along with my description of the abandoned mine where the boys discover a huge hoard of stolen valuables worth millions.

Flashback involves time travel of a different kind, as Max journeys back into someone else's life with the help of a psychic. Although Max only travels back twenty years to become David Dexter, research was still required into the world of the mid 1990s. To many of us this isn't that long ago and yet the world was very different in some ways back then, particularly in terms of technology and the way in which the online world is now such a big part of our daily lives. In 1995 everyone didn't have a mobile phone, no one was texting, there was no social media, and the internet was nowhere near as developed as it is today. Today a character might automatically look up an address or search for information on a website or on their phone but in the middle of the 1990s they'd have to use a phone book. Even though the time period in *Flashback* is relatively recent, research was just as important as it is when composing a story that takes place centuries ago.

Chapter Six
Researching eras:
Medieval medicine

I did a great deal of research into the world of medieval medicine when writing *The Heretic's Tomb*. This was essential in order to accurately describe not only the plague itself but also the wide range of methods used to combat the disease and the degree of medical knowledge that existed in 1349. The following details also appear on my website on pages featuring the historical background to *The Heretic's Tomb*.

The Middle Ages are often seen as a shadowy period of limited medical knowledge and great superstition. But many ideas from the classical medicine of the ancient Greeks and Romans survived into the medieval period relatively intact. Medical knowledge also arrived in Europe from the Arab world over the centuries, and doctors were familiar with the medicinal properties of some plants. However, treatments and cures were often as much to do with magic and superstition as they were associated with real medicine.

Doctors were very much guided by astrology in the Middle Ages. The Church, which influenced so much of medieval life, strongly disapproved of astrology, but found it difficult to stamp out. During the worst period of the Black Death, astrological charts became even more important for doctors. As the illness reached a noticeable crisis point, after which a patient either recovered or died, the time of recovery and the position of the stars and planets were seen as very significant. Even Guy de Chauliac, physician to three popes in succession, and author of the leading work on medieval surgery, was a firm believer in astrology. For operations, he would use recognized anesthetic potions, but also recommended bleeding and other procedures based on the position of the planets. Illnesses were also determined to be serious or not depending on whether they were under the sun's or the moon's influence.

As far as medicines were concerned, many medieval concoctions were little more than witch's brews. One of the best-known medicinal drugs of the Middle Ages was treacle or theriac, a blend of sixty-four different drugs in honey. Sold as a cure all, it was claimed to heal fevers, prevent internal swellings, clear skin blemishes, help with heart trouble, dropsy, epilepsy, and palsy, assist with sleep, aid digestion, strengthen limbs, heal wounds, and of course, cure the plague. Doctors at the time did make use of herbal remedies too. However, here again astrology had a distinct influence. The genuine medical properties of some plants were also related to how, and by whom, they were collected. Betony had to be picked by a small child in August before sunrise, and marigold when the moon had entered the house of Virgo. A herbalist also had to recite the proper designated prayers when preparing the medicine.

And yet, medieval doctors were also skilled at a variety of medical procedures. They could set broken bones, extract teeth, take out bladder stones, remove cataracts, and restored a scarred face by skin grafts from the arm. They knew that apoplexy and epilepsy were related to the brain. Urine samples, feces, and pulse rates were used to analyze ailments, and doctors were aware of which substances were diuretics and laxatives. It was also firmly believed that prevention was better than cure and great emphasis was placed on a healthy lifestyle, in which diet, exercise, mental attitude, and reduced stress all played a part.

Surgery was practiced in the Middle Ages too, although it was seen as a last resort. It is known to have been successful in the treatment of breast cancer, gangrene, hemorrhoids, and other conditions. There are illustrations showing medieval surgery, but naturally they give no indication of the pain suffered by the person on the operating table.

Anesthetics were used, but many of the concoctions used to relieve pain or induce sleep were also potentially fatal. Dwale, for example, consisted of gall from a cow or castrated boar, lettuce, briony, opium, henbane, and hemlock juice mixed with wine. The opium, alcohol, and hemlock would have made the patient incapable. Henbane and briony would have quickened the passage of poisons out of the body. However, it must be noted that hemlock was particularly dangerous, with too much being a death sentence.

Despite their skills and knowledge, for diseases and ailments beyond their abilities doctors fell back on solutions that seem bizarre to the modern reader. Ringworm was treated by washing the patient's hair in a boy's urine. Gout could be relieved by a plaster of goat dung mixed with rosemary and honey. Bloodletting was also popular as a cure for just about everything, with many different parts of the body used. For example, the two veins in the neck were to be tapped for leprosy, while the basilic vein, just below the elbow was said to clear the liver and spleen of any impurities.

If everything failed, charms, sacred relics, and incantations were used to ease the pain of childbirth, help contraception, cure toothache, remove boils, and even mend broken arms and legs. Medical knowledge eventually improved, but not immediately and for centuries to come, doctors were still very much influenced by superstition in the performance of their duties.

Chapter Seven
Characters

A time travel story might be set far into the future or in the distant past. Yet even if the setting is very different to the world in which your readers go about their daily lives, readers will be much more interested if they're able to compare the story to their own experiences. This may seem unlikely when dealing with the time travel genre. After all, traveling through time to a prehistoric era, Ancient Egypt, a medieval battlefield, Elizabethan England, the French Revolution, or hurtling thousands of years into the future certainly aren't everyday occurrences for most people.

Despite this, if the characters face common challenges in a time travel story the reader will find it much easier to relate to them. The lead characters might be ordinary people that have an extraordinary adventure, but they also need regular lives, jobs, friends, families, pets, work colleagues, bills to pay, and so on. Readers are more likely to finish your story if they're able to identify with the characters. Your characters need a personality, hobbies and interests, occupations or school life, a backstory of some kind, loved ones, likes and dislikes, motivations, personality quirks, all the kinds of things that make them come alive for the reader. If you can succeed in doing this well the reader is all the more likely to believe the amazing time travel journey that the characters undertake in the novel.

Let's imagine that you've thought of a great premise for a story and even crafted a general plot. You then need to develop some characters to inhabit the world you're intending to create. So where do ideas for characters come from? How do successful authors invent people for their stories, those imaginary men, women, children, and even animals that are a perfect fit for the story?

Ideas for characters can come from just about anywhere – on the train, street, plane, TV, movies, pictures and photographs, historical figures, or they can even be a composite of different people such as friends, family, neighbours, or work colleagues. However, if you've described a person in terms of their height, weight, general body type, hair and eye colour, age and clothing, this isn't really creating a character. All you have are the mere basics without any real meaning. This might as well be a life-size cardboard cutout rather than a character that appears to be a real person. Characters have to be realistic so that the reader will identify with them.

If the people in the story have what appears to be an ordinary life it makes the characters more plausible to the reader. Harry Potter's school at Hogwarts may not closely resemble the kind of educational institution that most children attend but the author made Harry a less than perfect student that struggles in certain classes. Most children don't attend boarding schools where they only go home in the winter or summer holidays and they certainly aren't educated in the ways of magic. Yet Harry's struggles still serve to make him more authentic as a character.

The best writers create characters that you instantly feel that you'd recognize on the street if they came to life. Think of the characters that you're familiar with from books to determine how good a job the author did when these creations were adapted for the screen. If we consider Harry Porter again, was your impression of the characters' appearance the same before the movies as it was when you saw the actors portraying them?

So what kinds of things make us different? Everyone doesn't like the same food and some are allergic to certain things. People are sometimes described as dog people or cat people but some might be neither or be allergic to dogs, cats, or both, affecting their choice of pets. We all have different likes and dislikes, or specific hopes and fears, things that help to determine our personality. People's voices are often distinctive, stereotypical male villains might stroke a beard thoughtfully, some people hug when they meet, others shy away from such close personal contact, some people have firm handshakes while some are very weak. These things and countless others comprise our personalities, differentiate us from our fellow humans, and make us who we are.

However, don't be tempted to make a character too different. Assuming that you're not creating a wacky cartoon character, don't invent someone with bright orange spiky hair, an eye patch, two facial scars in unusual shapes, a hooked hand, a wooden leg, and an unintelligible dialect, since this will not only seem ridiculous to the reader but also risk detracting from the telling of the story. And yet you also can't go too far in the opposite direction and make people too perfect, no matter how tempting that may be. After all, how many of us know any perfect people? Characters need problems, flaws, or phobias, whether these concern spiders, heights, crowds, closed spaces, or indeed anything that makes them more credible.

A good exercise is to invent your fictional character based on a picture. Creating a facial description is relatively simple, although you also need to determine if the person is tall or short, their body type, approximate age, and so on. You then need to add as much information as possible about this person, such as their personality, mannerisms, career path, the people that they interact with, their hopes and dreams, hobbies, pets, favourite foods and drinks, what part of the world they live in, the type of house they have or the car they drive, even where they went on holiday last year. All these will help to bring your character to life. The imaginary people in your stories will also need names, which usually conjure up specific images for the reader. This topic is covered in detail in the first installment of *The Children's Writer's Guide*.

The characters in your time travel novel can be entirely imaginary or they can be real people from history. However, whether they once existed or are purely fictional, the characters still need to be ones that the reader can understand. Characters also need to behave in a realistic manner and in a way that's appropriate for the time period depicted in the story. You can use a well-known character from history in your story, such as Julius Caesar, Cleopatra, Genghis Khan, Columbus, Leonardo Da Vinci, Michelangelo,

Elizabeth I, Napoleon, or Churchill. This will be more appealing to the reader. Even if these figures aren't the main characters in your story, you can create fictional characters that interact with them.

In *The Sorcerer's Letterbox*, Jack travels back to 1483 and meets Edward V and Richard III in the Tower of London. I undertook research into both characters to ensure that they were accurately represented in the story. It was also important to make sure that Richard III could conceivably have been present in the Tower of London at the time the story is set. If you include a real historical character in a scene that takes place on a date when this particular individual wasn't in London, out of the country, or had even already died, your story will lack credibility, to say the least. The other characters in the novel, such as Tyler, Meg, and the other outlaws are accurate representations of people that would have lived at the time. In *The Heretic's Tomb*, Lady Isabella Devereaux, Will, Sir Roger de Walsingham, Fitzwalter, Skerne, the abbess, and others are fictional but are based on plausible medieval characters. They also act and speak in a manner that's appropriate for England in 1349.

Dialogue is an essential part of every story. It moves the plot forward and builds characterization. Dialogue not only livens up a scene, but the way they talk to each other can reveal many things about your characters. As in stories with contemporary settings, the dialogue of the characters in a particular historical period in time travel stories can help us to learn more about them and also move the story along. Dialogue must be broadly in keeping with the era, but not so much that it becomes difficult for the reader to understand. Dialogue should also reflect the knowledge and thoughts of people in that time period. As I mentioned when discussing historical research, in the late Middle Ages, people in England spoke Middle English, which was not identical to the English that's spoken today. Written versions of this language appear in both *The Sorcerer's Letterbox* and *The Heretic's Tomb* although the dialogue spoken by the characters is composed so that the modern reader can understand it.

Novels, plays, and contemporary accounts of events can help writers to understand the dialogue of their chosen era. There are plenty of examples from the seventeenth, eighteenth, and early nineteenth centuries, as well as from the Victorian era and the twentieth century. We can obtain an impression of how the inhabitants of Ancient Greece or Imperial Rome may have talked from their surviving literature, but this is sometimes simply guesswork. Work composed in Old English or Middle English in the medieval period, such as the works of Chaucer, reveal the language of the time, but using this in your dialogue for medieval characters would make your story very difficult for your readers to understand. Shakespeare's plays also give us an insight into the Elizabethan and Jacobean period. However, it's not advisable to use this in the dialogue of characters inhabiting the world of the late sixteenth and early seventeenth centuries in your novel for the same reason.

Dialogue in scenes taking place in an earlier historical era has to be easy for the reader to understand so that they can follow the story.

However, there are still ways to ensure that the dialogue doesn't sound too modern and therefore out of place. For example, the use of contractions should be avoided in dialogue for characters interacting in the medieval period. While this may not be entirely historically accurate it does give the characters a more authentic feel. For example, "I don't think they'll dare to attack the castle again before it gets dark" doesn't sound as much in keeping with the Middle Ages as "I do not think that they will dare to attack the castle again before nightfall." Think of movies that are set in different historical periods. The dialogue usually sounds like we'd expect, even if this isn't always historically correct.

It's also important to make sure that you don't put thoughts into people's heads or concepts into their dialogue that are alien to that time period. It can be tempting to slip modern beliefs or assumptions into your character's speech, but this will detract from the authenticity of your historical setting. The same applies to the dialogue used by your modern characters in the past. In most time travel stories or movies people always seem to speak English, whether they're in Ancient Rome, on Viking ships, or in countless other time periods. Obviously this is done so that people will be able to understand what's being said but writers must try not to use modern speech for their characters when they're talking to people from another era since this will often turn off the reader. It's similar to the employment of anachronisms, when items such as mechanical devices or types of clothing are introduced into an era before they were invented.

These considerations regarding dialogue can also apply to stories that feature travel into the future but there are no established rules about this. We can assume that some words in common use today will be antiques in the future while other words and phrases will have been invented which we're currently unfamiliar with. Think of the words that have become part of the English language just in the last few years, mostly associated with computers and the internet. These include upload, download, blog, Wi-Fi, cell phone, and so many others. Some simple words such as text have become verbs while Google is now a euphemism for searching for something online. It's a fair bet that human languages will continue to evolve and that in a future setting there will be words that doesn't exist today. How often you use those will depend on how much effort you want to put into world building for a story set in the future. It might also depend on how far into the future your story is set. If it's only fifty years things might not have altered too much but if the story takes place thousands of years ahead, things might be very different. However, the same rules, if they can be called that, still apply since the time traveling characters might escape or be on the run and their speech could give reveal their true identities. It all depends how important this element is to you as a writer when creating your story but it's something to consider so that you retain the reader's interest right to the end.

When choosing names for your characters that inhabit a specific period, it's very important to select names that would have been in use in that era. Popular male names in the Middle Ages included Edward, John, Henry, Richard, Robert,

Roger, Thomas, or William. Female names included familiar ones such as Anne, Elizabeth, Mary, or Margaret, but also names that are rarely seen today, such as Edith, Joan, or Matilda. In *The Sorcerer's Letterbox*, Jack is the main character, since I needed a name that's used today that would also have been popular in the Middle Ages. Jack's friend in 1483 is called Meg, another appropriate name for the time period. In *The Heretic's Tomb*, Annie is a name that's familiar today but would also have been in use in 1349. Her partner during the era of the Black Death is Will, another common medieval name. Lady Isabella Devereaux was inspired by Queen Isabella, the wife of Edward II, who lived several decades earlier than the setting of the story. The main villain is Sir Roger de Walsingham, who has a name that also wouldn't sound out of place in the mid-fourteenth century. However, you still need to thoroughly research your preferred names. Although you're not going to use a modern name for a medieval character, if you're story's set in 1300 you also need to avoid using names that weren't popular until more than a hundred years later.

Whatever historical period features in your story, if your characters are well drawn, appear to be realistic and easily identified with, have appropriate names, and use period dialogue, your time travel story will be all the more effective.

Chapter Eight
Telling your story

In numerous classic time travel tales, the hero journeys into the past or future only to discover that their machine or device has either malfunctioned, broken, is out of power, or has been stolen by the chief villains of the piece. This leads to an adventure in which the main character is stranded and a story in which time travel itself, along with all its complexities, is the key element.

As with stories set in the present day, the plot of your time travel story has to make sense, be plausible, and involve a solution to a problem. The plots in time travel stories usually feature both fictional and true events. Fictional events are those that involve your characters, whether these are ones that you've invented for the story or historical figures that you've chosen to use as part of the narrative. Real events are of course things that happened in your chosen time period that affect how you tell your time travel tale. Even if the main character is moving through a world that existed long ago, he or she still needs to have a goal and this needs to be established as early as possible. It also has to be important to the character otherwise it's not going to appear to be crucial to the reader either, who simply won't bother turning the page.

Things need to keep changing for the main character as the story progresses. If they're in the same basic position at the end of the chapter as they were when it began, what was the point of telling the story of that episode? The plot has to keep moving, in whatever way is best for your particular story, otherwise it might as well be a shopping list. Pacing is crucial if you're going to retain the reader's attention. Cliffhangers at the end of your chapters will also always make the reader want to learn more.

No matter how good an idea you think you have, if the reader can't follow the plot early on in the novel they're not going to continue reading.

Some writers of time travel stories get too bogged down in the detail of the historical period, in describing the surrounding scenery, the clothing or weapons, or focus too much on the events of the time, whether these play a major role in the story or not. You might be fascinated by your chosen era and an expert on everything related to the time period, but there still has to be a storyline when composing any work of fiction, even if it concerns something as complex as time travel.

The descriptions of characters, locations, and events need to be very vivid in the historical sections of time travel stories. Important historical information that the reader may be unfamiliar with also needs to be well explained. However, don't be tempted to include too much detail, since this will interfere with the flow of the story. You may be an enthusiast about eighteenth century sailing ships, but don't assume that the reader is similarly fascinated by your descriptions of ropes, masts, and rigging. Just give the reader enough to create a picture in their mind so that they can visualize the characters in this setting that you've created.

In *The Alchemist's Portrait*, Matthew travels to several different time periods. While he isn't in any of these eras for that long, it was still important to set the scene for the reader so that they could visualize in their own mind what the main character was viewing. This could involve describing a character's appearance and clothing when Matthew appears in Paris in 1792, the type of rifle the villain is carrying in the American Civil War episode, or the surrounding area when Matthew arrives in the middle of St. Petersburg during the Russian Revolution.

In *The Sorcerer's Letterbox* and *The Heretic's Tomb*, medieval scenes, whether of rural villages or the city of London, needed to be described just enough without risking the reader losing interest. Some readers might be familiar with the Tower of London and have visited the location in recent years. However, in *The Sorcerer's Letterbox*, the description of how the complex looked in 1483 was very important to the story since important sections of the plot take place there. London Bridge was the only way to cross the Thames for many years during the medieval period. Consequently this was a major feature of the city during the Middle Ages and the bridge is also described in detail in the novel.

The Doomsday Mask isn't a time travel adventure but does include scenes portraying an earlier historical period. Most of the story takes place in a contemporary setting but the first part of the novel is set in Berlin and the surrounding area in the last days of World War II. The descriptions of the city and its destruction during the intense fighting had to be accurate, as well as the depictions of the very young soldiers that were recruited to defend Berlin against the Soviet forces. This part of the story is brief but still very important in order to set the scene and include elements that prepare the reader for what comes next.

In *Flashback*, Max only travels back in time a couple of decades but his surroundings still needed to be described correctly. When he's living as David Dexter in the mid 1990s, Max notices differences in hairstyles, clothing, the types of cars on the street, and other everyday occurrences which initially might not seem overly important but are crucial factors in portraying the time period as accurately as possible. There's less background music emanating from overhead speakers, no one using laptops in coffee shops, and everyone isn't talking, texting, or playing games on their mobile phone. People were also still allowed to smoke in many public places, even in some restaurants, all of which needed to be depicted accurately in the novel. In *Future Imperfect*, although Alexander sends Alex and Stephanie messages from his own time, the main characters view images from several decades in the future rather than traveling forward in time in person. However, these futuristic scenes still had to be described in detail since they're an integral part of the story and also have to be believable to the reader.

Any novelist, whether they're writing for children or adults, must invent a complete imagined world in which the characters live and the creation of realistic settings is a key element in any story. If your novel features imaginary scientific facilities, such as laboratories or sophisticated control rooms, the technology might be fictional but the setting still has to be described vividly enough to consistently capture the imagination of the reader, even if they're very familiar with these types of places from other books, movies and TV shows. If some of the story's action takes place in a particular building or structure, which may or may not resemble something that we'd see today, the author has to include detailed descriptions of any working technology and how the characters interact, not only with each other, but also with their surroundings.

Time travel stories, whether they involve mechanical devices or magic, require a great deal of imagination and there are often some very complex issues to grapple with before you even start writing the novel. While creating your time travel method and making it plausible to the reader are very important, this doesn't mean that you can neglect the story. Your time travel novel might be a work of fantasy but you still have to craft a plot that makes sense and create a well-written story with believable settings that keeps the reader engaged right to the end.

Chapter Nine
The trouble with time travel

Time travel stories are full of complications that the author needs to be aware of when writing their story. There are also issues that need to be dealt with so that the story doesn't confuse the reader or make them dislike your book altogether. Lots of so-called rules have been established in time travel stories over the years, some of which contradict each other or sometimes don't seem to make sense, if time travel ever really does. I'll not attempt to go into them all here but let's examine a few examples of issues that illustrate the trouble with time travel.

We looked at the butterfly effect in an earlier section of the book. This implies that even the slightest of changes to the past could have dire consequences for the future. In quite a few stories in the genre, a traveler journeys back to a certain point in history to attempt to do something good, either at an earlier stage in their own life or at a critical point in history, but instead creates a nightmare present for himself when he returns to his own time. In other stories the changes to the past are accidental or not even noticed at the time, as in Bradbury's *A Sound of Thunder*, when the death of butterfly in the distant past sets a course of events in motion that results in the travelers returning to an altered present.

The movie *12 Monkeys* mentions the Cassandra Complex. This term is originally from Greek mythology, in which the prophet Cassandra refused the advances of Apollo. As a result, Apollo cursed her so that no one would believe her predictions. Cassandra could therefore see the future and try to warn people of disasters to come but couldn't change the course of events or get others to believe her. In terms of time travel, this means that no matter how much the time traveler needs to convince people in the past to change something so that a horrible future won't come to pass, no one believes him and thinks that he's crazy. After all, time travel is impossible, right? Even if someone claims to be traveling from the future to prove that it exists. Some people believe that the absence of time travelers from the future is proof that time travel is impossible. And yet perhaps they really are here, observing us like tourists while keeping their true identities secret.

Sometimes people are able to change events and affect history but only if they tinker with the past life of someone unimportant. In the original series of *Star Trek*, in the episode *Tomorrow is Yesterday* the Enterprise accidentally captures a pilot who then gains knowledge of the future, which could affect his present. Complicated, isn't it? Although the pilot doesn't seem to be that crucial to history, Kirk and Spock learn that his son, who isn't even born at that point, is destined to lead a space mission to Saturn. In *The City On The Edge Of Forever* when a woman's life is saved by McCoy in the 1930s, history is altered, leading to a German victory in World War II and a chain of events that cancels out the existence of the Enterprise in the future. Only traveling back in time and the death of the woman can put what

Kirk and the others know as history back on track. In *Back to the Future,* when Marty changes his parents' lives in the past, he starts to fade away since he'll have never existed. Only by taking action to ensure that his parents become a couple does he guarantee that he survives.

Sometimes people go back in time but they always did. Let's think about that one for a moment. What this means is that you were always destined to travel back in time and whatever actions you take were already part of the timeline anyway. In the *Star Trek: The Next Generation* episode *Time's Arrow,* the cast members travel back to San Francisco in the nineteenth century to make things happen in the way they're supposed to do. Thus although they aren't from that time, they were already part of events which couldn't have unfolded in the way they did without their journey from the future. Once again, this illustrates how time travel is a complex business but although these concepts are entirely fictional, time travel writers have a lot of fun while refining their plotlines.

Earlier we also looked at the grandfather

paradox, which would appear to make time travel completely impossible if someone could kill their ancestors and prevent their own birth. Many believe that the past can't be changed, which would prevent this paradox from occurring at all, but that hasn't stopped time travel writers from having characters go into the past to alter history, both for good and for bad.

Tinkering with past events might sometimes seem like a good idea but this is often oversimplified and doesn't consider the many other events that were happening at the time that all interacted with each other. World War II and the rise of Hitler are classic examples of this kind of thinking. Some writers speculate that if Hitler had been killed as a baby, during his childhood, as a young man in World War I, or even during the early 1920s before his rise to power, World War II would never have happened. The conditions in Germany in the early 1930s were ripe for someone like Hitler to arrive on the scene so who knows if someone else might have appeared that was worse or just as bad as Hitler. The war might still have happened and the

Holocaust might still have occurred too, if someone with similar ideas to Hitler had taken control of Germany, leading to similar if not identical consequences.

There's also the possibility that the Soviet Union might have invaded Central and Western Europe in the late 1930s. Without the large American military presence that that existed on the continent after 1945 the Red Army might well have succeed. This isn't such a far-fetched idea when you consider the indecision of British and French leaders toward Hitler before war broke out over Poland in 1939. And of course preventing Hitler's rise to power does nothing to prevent Japanese expansion in Asia and the Pacific. And finally more than 60 million died in World War II and if all those people had lived who knows if one of them would have ended up being worse than Hitler? Some time travel stories try to explain the paradoxes in the sense that things can be changed but create a whole new timeline. This presupposes that there are an infinite number of timelines in existence somewhere, which we'll look in more detail in the final chapter.

If you do have characters attempting to change the past, either to affect their own life or major historical events, the writer has to make sure that the story's continuity holds up to scrutiny. Even if the changes were for the better, everything worked out, and the traveler's mission was a success, there are still going to be some changes in the present day. In *Flashback*, Max's journey is successful and results in a different reality for some of the characters in the story, including himself. Although Max retains his knowledge of the different timelines, other people don't have the same ability. As a result, it was very important to determine which characters knew what once the timeline had been adjusted. For example, although Max knows everyone in the story that he encounters, even those that have threatened him in the past, some of them have never met him and so couldn't know certain things. This caused considerable problems when writing the three books in the series but I worked it all out in the end and hopefully produced a very compelling story.

85

When Harry and Hermione use the time-turner in *The Prisoner of Azkaban* they have to be careful not to see themselves or let their past selves see them when they're on their rescue mission to the past. This issue is also mentioned in the *Back to the Future* movies, where Marty has to avoid being seen, although in the second movie his partner Jennifer faints when she sees another version of herself. In *Timecop* the villain of the story dissolves when he comes into contact with his other self from the future.

As you can see, there are lots of rules that have been invented over the years regarding time travel but none are carved in stone. The basic message seems to be, if you can make your time travel method appear plausible and the idea doesn't have any holes that the readers can criticize, go for it. Sometimes characters seem to be able to use time travel to solve one problem but not another, something that is rarely explained. Some stories also mention fixed points in time that can't ever be changed. These are sometimes chosen at random but the implication is that some key moments in history might be somehow off limits to the time traveler in terms of preventing or altering them in some way because the consequences would be too far reaching in the years and decades that followed.

When writing time travel stories, anachronisms need to be avoided. Fictional characters in the medieval period or in World War II obviously can't carry cell phones, check their email, or talk about TV shows. However, characters also can't have political views that aren't in keeping with their time, level of education, or social status. The role of women in society was also often very different at certain times in the past. Female heroines in historical fiction are often depicted in ways designed to appeal to modern audiences. Their anachronistic attitudes to a woman's role in society may help readers to relate to them, but this is very much out of step with how women were treated in the eighteenth or nineteenth century, for example. Similarly the author may give a medieval peasant or a Roman slave political views that are utterly out of place with the character's time period.

Sometimes an author includes an element in

their story that they assume existed in their chosen period but hadn't been invented or discovered at that time. For example, someone might be shown eating potatoes in a medieval English castle although Europeans didn't discover potatoes until after the voyages of Columbus, beginning in 1492. It's also important to show characters using appropriate firearms for a particular period, such as a rifle or a musket. And while outlaws in the Old West may have used revolvers, pirates sailing the Caribbean two hundred years earlier would not.

Your lead character from the era of the Napoleonic Wars shouldn't wake up in the morning to his electrical alarm clock, check his text messages, zip up his pants, and have waffles for breakfast, but make sure he's a true fit for his era in many other ways too.

Chapter Ten
Time travel into the future

We're all very familiar with stories about time travel to the past, perhaps wondering what it would be like to witness historical events, meet famous people, or perhaps being tempted to change the things that took place. However, some time travel stories have featured journeys into the future. The methods used to travel into the future are often very similar to those used in stories featuring journeys into the past, such as machinery, advanced technology, magic, jewelry, handheld devices, items that are ingested, and even spaceships traveling at incredible speeds. The writer has to create an entire imagined world in the future, which can often be a challenge but also great fun to write.

We already mentioned *The Time Machine* by H G Wells, in which the traveler visits an era tens of thousands of years in the future. There he witnesses the potential consequences of human evolution and mankind's social systems but it's a world he barely recognizes as his own. When people travel to the past, research is required to make sure that the events, people, and settings are all depicted accurately, as we covered in the chapter about historical research. When people travel to the future the writer is able to create whatever kind of world they want but this still has to be plausible and the plot has to make sense. There are also issues to consider when people travel from the future into the present, as detailed in the previous chapter.

In the original *Planet of the Apes* movie, astronauts led by George Taylor, played by Charlton Heston, embark on a long space voyage in 1972. The crewmembers have been placed in deep hibernation so that they only age eighteen months during the lengthy journey. When the ship crashes on what appears to be an unknown planet, the ship's instruments show the date as 3978, more than two thousand years after the crew set off. The astronauts have traveled far into the future to an era when intelligent apes rule Earth. In the iconic scene at the end of the movie, when Taylor sees the ruined Statue of Liberty on the beach, he realizes that humans devastated the planet in a nuclear war. This allowed the apes to become the dominant species and replace mankind. The idea spawned other movies and a TV series, which also featured time travel, most notably when the apes traveled from the future to our time.

H G Wells' *The Time Machine* from 1895 envisaged a distant future while his novel *The Shape of Things to Come*, published in 1933, portrayed an imaginary history of the world from that time until 2106. Fritz Lang's movie *Metropolis* was released in 1927 and while not involving time travel has its own vision of the Earth set in an imaginary world one hundred years in the future. *1984* by George Orwell features a nightmare totalitarian world that would probably have seemed very possible when Orwell wrote the book in 1948, in the aftermath of World War II around the beginning of the Cold War.

In the first half of the twentieth century there were other examples of writers and artists imaging what the future might be like, envisaging flying cars, airships, space travel, examples of highly advanced technology, and goodness knows what else. Images from these times often appear on websites as retrofuture images and while not related to time travel they reveal how people imagined what might come to pass in their future. In some stories depicting travel to the future the characters live on another planet in the solar system, on the moon, or somewhere else in space because the Earth has become uninhabitable. However, this setting still has to be well described by the writer even if it's only a few decades in the future. The time travel writer can invent as comprehensive a world as he or she likes or simply employ selected examples from an imaginary future, including just enough detail to make the story work.

Human cloning has been the topic of many stories, TV shows, and movies over the years and has appeared in some stories about imaginary futures. Although the benefits of the technology are debated today, cloning could perhaps be applied to current medical procedures or used to combat incurable diseases and medical conditions. Writers might envisage other potential future medical inventions that currently seem like science fiction. Writers also sometimes explore potential inventions that might utterly transform the way we live in the coming decades.

Even when inventing a futuristic world that's completely fictional, the writer also has to create an imaginary timeline that preceded the era that they've created. This is particularly true when a story is only set a few decades ahead of the present day. If the story takes place thousands of years in the future, full details of everything that happened in the imaginary preceding timeline don't always need to be fully explained. If the story takes place twenty or thirty years from now, the writer needs to tell us all about the different things that happened up to that point. Some of these details can seem very logical, based on the potential consequences of selected current or recent events in the author's own time. Once some of these imaginary previous timelines have been created this opens up the possibility of alternate timelines and histories, which we'll explore in the next chapter.

If the story is set thousands of years in the future, the technology that's employed by the human race in imaginary time can seem completely fantastical and well beyond anything that might exist today. This is of course if the future world is not depicted as a smoking ruin as a result of nuclear war, biological epidemics, or is a dystopian society devoid of law and order. This type of theme has appeared in many movies and stories over the years and remains popular. If the story doesn't take place too far ahead of the era when the writer is creating the story the general setting, such as buildings, scenery, any technology that still exists, even clothing, can be similar to what we'd see today. Time travel stories that involve journeys to the future can be just as imaginative, if not more so, than stories that feature traveling into the past, where the events are already recorded and are easy to research by those that may wonder if the writer's portrayal of a historical period is accurate. However, even though a future scenario is derived entirely from the author's imagination it still has to be plausible and the story still has to be good if the reader is expected to enjoy it.

Time travel into the future has been made possible in movies, TV series, and books by a variety of methods. In *Star Trek* time travel into the future has been made possible by wormholes, tears in the space-time continuum, incredible speeds, alien devices, and other means, including journeys into alternate futures, which we'll explore in the following chapter. In *The Door into Summer* Dan Davis travels into the future after being frozen in suspended animation, something that has often featured in time travel stories. Sometimes the freezing device malfunctions and the person sleeps for much longer than expected. In the second *Back to the Future* movie, Marty uses the De Lorean to travel to 2015, which was of course thirty years in the future from when the adventure was set in the mid 1980s.

In my novel *The Time Camera*, the device at the center of the story is capable of taking pictures and video of the past. Scientists are also in the process of capturing images further and further back in time. In the course of their work they realize that the camera is also capable of taking images and video of the future. This involves viewing the future rather than traveling forward in time but Magnus Sinclair, the villain of the story, is still able to use his knowledge of the future to enrich himself by viewing newspaper headlines and stock market information in advance. In *Flashback*, Max travels back into someone else's body in the mid 1990s, outwardly becoming that person for a brief period, but of course still has knowledge of the future, which he's able to use to his advantage in 1995. However, Max still has to be careful not to make changes that will adversely affect the future.

In *Future Imperfect*, Alex and Stephanie receive messages on Alex's phone from the future, encouraging them to take certain actions so that terrible events won't occur. This may seem like a very noble idea but the reader, and indeed the characters, are left in suspense regarding whether the messages from the future are genuine. Alex and Stephanie also wonder if the messages from the future are simply a trick by someone who might be trying to get them to act in a certain way in the present so that the disastrous future does in fact unfold. Sound complicated? It certainly is. Whether you're dealing with time travel to the future or into the past, the genre can be very complex and the writer always has to take a great deal of care when creating a story.

Characters traveling to the past have to be careful that the knowledge of the future doesn't adversely affect the timeline, unless that's part of their mission when journeying to an earlier era. People that travel to the future also have knowledge that could be harmful when they return to their own time. This was explored in some episodes of the original *Star Trek* series and also in *Star Trek: The Next Generation*, as well as in a number of other stories. Sometimes people travel to the future or witness events that haven't yet occurred in order to influence the course of history. Of course if they were able to invent a machine that provided knowledge of what was to come this implies that the future is fluid and can always be changed by manipulation of things in our time. If the future that the traveler witnessed can be changed by an action in the present then that particular version of the future never really existed. This leads nicely into a discussion about alternate realities, parallel universes, and alternate timelines, which should be mentioned in any discussion about time travel stories.

Chapter Eleven
Alternate history

Writers are allowed a certain amount of artistic license when creating a time travel story, but mustn't deviate from the known historical facts if they're used as a backdrop or as an integral part of the plot. Stories that do stray from the established timeline are classed as alternate history or are sometimes called "What if?" stories. These are usually set in a world where historic events either didn't occur or unfolded in a different way. Alternate history stories usually have a very important event as a point of divergence so that when changes are made they greatly affect what we know as history. These kinds of stories can also take place in parallel universes or indeed in any setting that the author devises.

For example, if Napoleon Bonaparte were

killed in battle in 1799, when military commanders were often in the thick of battle, history would have been dramatically changed. In that year Napoleon mounted his coup to take over the government, eventually becoming emperor of France. Had he died in 1799 the Napoleonic Wars would never have happened, since it's difficult to imagine those conflicts following the French Revolution happening without him. Yes, there may still have been a series of wars, since France and the other European powers were fighting for much of the 1790s. Yet without Napoleon's military genius French leaders might well have been overwhelmed and simply given up the crusade to spread their revolutionary ideals across Europe.

Another popular point of divergence is the American Civil War, in which the outcomes of some of the crucial battles are changed and the Confederacy is the eventual victor in the conflict. In reality, the Confederacy was hopelessly outmatched by the Union as the war went on, in terms of manpower, industrialization, railroads, population, and the size of the army it could put into the field. It seems unlikely that the Confederacy could have won the Civil War but a Southern victory would certainly have changed events in the decades that followed. Perhaps the most popular topic in alternate history is a German victory in World War II and how this might have transformed the course of history. *Fatherland* by Robert Harris is set in 1964 when Nazi Germany rules Europe and is engaged in a Cold War with the United States. In Philip K. Dick's *The Man in the High Castle* Germany and Japan won World War II and divided North America between them.

If the Roman Empire had never risen to prominence the consequences would have been far reaching, even up until the present day. In another alternative scenario, what would the world have looked like if the empire had remained intact into the modern era? Some writers have explored the idea that the Spanish Armada conquered Elizabethan England in 1588 or speculated what might have happened had Columbus not discovered the New World in 1492. Perhaps the asteroid impact that eliminated the dinosaurs never occurred or had a much less destructive effect. Would dinosaurs then have evolved as mammals did, filling a gap in the ecosystem? It's certainly intriguing to think what might have happened had dinosaurs become bipedal creatures and lived much as modern humans do.

These kinds of alternate historical scenarios aren't really classified as time travel but do involve the author inventing imaginary worlds, often with real characters in different roles, taking different actions, dying at a different time and so on, so that they still have an impact on history. And of course fictional characters might be joined by minor personalities from that historical period that step forward to play a larger role in events as a result of the differences that the author has created in the timeline.

Alternate history deals with the idea that individuals, groups, or events in the established historical timeline can be presented in a different way to create an alternate reality. Writers have also explored this idea on an individual basis for characters in stories. For example, many in the scientific community now accept the existence of parallel universes as a possibility. I mentioned earlier that if time travel is possible perhaps previous events can't be changed due to time travel paradoxes. Yet there's also the theory that history can indeed be changed and if this takes place an alternate timeline or parallel universe is then created.

If a time traveler cancels out their own existence they couldn't have gone back in time in the first place, making the entire concept of time travel impossible. However, if another timeline is created if changes are made, the original timeline still exists and is simply in another parallel dimension. Think about this in terms of everyday life. For every action we take as individuals we often made a clear decision to do a certain thing. This could be as simple as crossing the street, choosing to stay with a friend for an extra cup of coffee, deciding to put on a certain pair of shoes, or even going to bed earlier than usual. Clearly we could easily have made a different choice that would have created a separate subsequent timeline. This obviously results in an almost unlimited number of timelines extending from each decision that's made. Further alternate timelines begin with any new decisions, leading to multiple parallel universes. If these all exist at the same time, perhaps travel into those universes is actually possible. While the number of these might be mind-boggling the notion serves as an excellent source of inspiration for writers of science fiction and fantasy stories.

Conclusion

Time travel is a complicated topic but the genre shows no signs of waning in popularity. Many of us also remain fascinated by history and some historical periods will probably always be used as the theme of books, movies, and TV shows. Science fiction remains popular too and there will no doubt continue to be many stories written about imaginary future eras.

As we've examined, writers of time travel stories not only have to create believable plots and invent plausible characters that the reader will identify with but also have unique challenges to deal with. These include conducting accurate historical research, the creation of authentic settings, and the crafting of dialogue that's appropriate for the time period. Authors also have to invent imaginary devices or methods of time travel that are clearly impossible but still need to appear to work. The writer's time travel adventure might also involve dealing with the effects of changing an established timeline, the use of historical characters, and time travel paradoxes.

Despite all this, writers in the genre always have a lot of fun when they're writing their stories, especially when inventing their time travel method, refining its operational details, or creating an entire imaginary world. There will always be more things to take care of when writing a time travel story but it's always worth it in the end, so take your time and enjoy the ride.

About the Author

Simon Rose's first novel for middle-grade readers, *The Alchemist's Portrait*, was published in 2003, followed by *The Sorcerer's Letterbox* in 2004, *The Clone Conspiracy* in 2005, *The Emerald Curse* in 2006, *The Heretic's Tomb* in 2007, *The Doomsday Mask* in 2009, *The Time Camera* in 2011, *The Sphere of Septimus* in 2014, *Flashback* in 2015, *Future Imperfect* in 2016, *Twisted Fate* and the *Shadowzone* series in 2017, *Parallel Destiny* in 2018, and *The Stone of the Seer* series in 2022.

Simon is also the author of *The Children's Writer's Guide*, *The Working Writer's Guide*, *The Social Media Writer's Guide*, *Where Do Ideas*

Come From?, The Time Traveler's Guide, The Children's Writer's Guide 2, a contributing author to *The Complete Guide to Writing Science Fiction,* and has written more than a hundred non-fiction books for children and young adults with Crabtree Publishing, Beech Street Books, True North, Capstone, and Weigl Educational Publishers.

Simon is a writing instructor at the University of Calgary, has served as the Writer-in-Residence for the Canadian Authors Association, and is a member of the Calgary Association of Freelance Editors. Simon provides editing, coaching, and coaching services for writers in a wide range of genres. You can view details of the references and recommendations regarding his work on his website.

Simon offers in-person and virtual programs for schools and libraries, and offers a variety of online writing courses and workshops for both children and adults. He has extensive experience in writing for a wide range of industries and offers copywriting services for the business community.

Full details can be found at his website, www.simon-rose.com.

Books by Simon Rose

Fiction

The Alchemist's Portrait

The Sorcerer's Letterbox

The Clone Conspiracy

The Emerald Curse

The Heretic's Tomb

The Doomsday Mask

The Time Camera

The Sphere of Septimus

Future Imperfect

Flashback

Twisted Fate

Parallel Destiny

Shadowzone

Into the Web

Black Dawn

The Stone of the Seer

Royal Blood

Revenge of the Witchfinder

Simon Rose

Non-fiction

The Time Traveler's Guide

Where Do Ideas Come From?

The Children's Writer's Guide

The Children's Writer's Guide 2

The Working Writer's Guide

The Social Media Writer's Guide

Exploring the Fantasy Realm

*School and Library Visits for Authors and
    Illustrators*

Amazing Animals: Belugas

Canadian Icons: Loonies

Remarkable People: Nelson Mandela

Canadian Icons: Canada's Olympic Torch

Meteors

Remarkable People: Aung San Suu Kyi

Sources of Light

What is Light?

Sea Urchins

Colosseum

Army

Navy

Air Force

Simon Rose

Canada in World War I: A Soldier's Life

Canada in World War I: Life at Home

Canada in World War I: The Aftermath

America at War: Civil War

America at War: Revolutionary War

America at War: War of 1812

America at War: Mexican-American War

The Cardiovascular System

The Nervous System

The Skeletal System

The Respiratory System

The Digestive System

The Muscular System

Senate: U.S. Government

House of Representatives: U.S. Government

Supreme Court: U.S. Government

The Presidency: U.S. Government

House of Commons: Canada's Government

Senate: Canada's Government

Supreme Court: Canada's Government

The Crown: Canada's Government

One World Trade Centre

Oriental Pearl

Drones: Global Issues

Simon Rose

Canadian Celebrations - Canada Day

Canadian Celebrations - Halloween

Tsunami Readiness

Earthquake Readiness

First Nations, Metis, and Inuit Governance

Responsibilities of Citizenship

Canada's Political Parties

Healthy Kids Canada: Personal Safety

Healthy Kids Canada: Substances

Healthy Kids Canada: Embracing

Healthy Kids Canada: Real and Fictional Violence

Healthy Kids Canada: Gender Identity

Healthy Kids Canada: Growth and Development

Indigenous Life in Canada: Search for Clean Water

Indigenous Life in Canada: Racism and Stereotypes

Indigenous Life in Canada: Development of the Reserve System

Indigenous Life in Canada: Housing and Infrastructure

*Indigenous Life in Canada: Missing and
    Exploited Indigenous Women and Girls*

*Indigenous Life in Canada: Employment and
    Education*

War in Afghanistan

Battle of Vimy Ridge

Battle of the Somme

Battle of Juno Beach

Battle of the Atlantic

Battle of the Plains of Abraham

Anthologies

*The Complete Guide to Writing Science
    Fiction Part One*

* List current as of October 2022

Made in United States
North Haven, CT
05 March 2023

33600741R00067